NATIONAL GEOGRAPHIC KiDS

MW00944609

Funny FiLL-IN

MY BACKYARD ADVENTURE

NATIONAL GEOGRAPHIC SOCIETY
WASHINGTON, D.C.

How to Play Funny Fill-In!

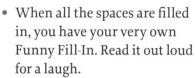

Love to create amazing stories? Good, because this one stars YOU. Get ready to laugh with all your friends—you can play with as many people as you want! Make sure to keep this book on your shelf. You'll want to read it again and again!

Are You Ready to Laugh?

- One person picks a story—you can start at the beginning, the middle, or the end of the book.

- Ask a friend to call out a word that the space asks for—noun, verb, or something else—and write it in the blank space. If there's more than one player, ask the next person to say a word. Extra points for creativity!

- When all the spaces are filled in, you have your very own Funny Fill-In. Read it out loud for a laugh.

- Want to play by yourself? Just fold over the page and use the cardboard insert at the back as a writing pad. Fill in the blank parts of speech list, and copy your answers into the story.

Make sure you check out the amazing **Fun Facts** that appear on every page!

Parts of Speech

To play the game, you'll need to know how to form sentences. This list with examples of the parts of speech and other terms will help you get started:

Noun: The name of a person, place, thing, or idea
Examples: tree, mouth, creature
*The **ocean** is full of colorful **fish**.*

Adjective: A word that describes a noun or pronoun
Examples: green, lazy, friendly
*My **silly** dog won't stop laughing!*

Verb: An action word. In the present tense, a verb often ends in –s or –ing. If the space asks for past tense, changing the vowel or adding a –d or –ed to the end usually will set the sentence in the past.
Examples: swim, hide, plays, running (present tense); biked, rode, jumped (past tense)
*The giraffe **skips** across the savanna.*
*The flower **opened** after the rain.*

Adverb: A word that describes a verb and usually ends in –ly
Examples: quickly, lazily, soundlessly
*Kelley **greedily** ate all the carrots.*

Plural: More than one
Examples: mice, telephones, wrenches
*Why are all the **doors** closing?*

Silly Word or Exclamation: A funny sound, a made-up word, a word you think is totally weird, or a noise someone or something might make
Examples: Ouch! No way! Foozleduzzle! Yikes!
*"**Darn!**" shouted Jim. "These cupcakes are sour!"*

Specific Words: There are many more ways to make your story hilarious. When asked for something like a number, animal, or body part, write in something you think is especially funny.

your age

adjective

animal

noun

same animal

game

food, plural

adjective

something soft

adverb ending in –ly

color

secret talent

noun

noun

color

noun

number

noun, plural

DON'T MISS the BONANZA

Annual Bonanza

I can't believe it! It's finally here! I've waited ___7___ years and it's finally here! I've been dreaming
 your age

of this day from the moment I became a member of the __stinky__ __bear__ Scouts
 adjective *animal*

when I was just a little __Lego__. This is the first year I get to go to the __bear__ Scout
 noun *same animal*

Bonanza! I can't wait to play __hot + cold__, roast __hot dogs__, participate in a(n) __good__
 game *food, plural* *adjective*

__pillow__ fight, and sing __badly__ around the campfire. Of course, the best
 something soft *adverb ending in –ly*

part is that I'm finally earning a(n) __green__ badge for my ability to __building legos__.
 color *secret talent*

Now, first things first—I have to figure out what to pack. Of course I'll need my __mama__ and
 noun

my __daddy__—oh, and I can't forget that __red__ __boat__!
 noun *color* *noun*

Better grab ___7___ __grasses__, too, just in case. Oh boy, this is going to be the
 number *noun, plural*

best weekend ever!

- noun
  - nickname
- large number
  - verb ending in –ing
- animal, plural
  - adjective
- noun
  - food
- adjective
  - noun
- fruit
  - body part
- body part, plural
  - adjective
- food, plural
  - verb
- noun, plural
  - animal, plural
- noun

Fun Fact! IN THE UNITED STATES ALONE, MORE THAN **40 MILLION** PEOPLE GO **CAMPING** EACH YEAR.

Brrrrinnngggg! The _____ rang so loud it made me jump! "I'll get it!" I called to my mom,
               noun

but she had already answered. A few minutes later I came downstairs. "I have bad news, _____,"
                                                                                        nickname

she said. "The bonanza is canceled. It seems that _____ _____ _____
                                                    large number   verb ending in –ing   animal, plural

got _____ and destroyed the campsite." "Noooo!" I cried. My fellow scouts will be so upset! No
     adjective

_____ races? No all-you-can-eat _____ contests? Not even one _____
noun   food   adjective

_____ ? I looked at Mom and frowned. "Cheer up, _____ _____ .
noun   fruit   body part

I have an idea!" she said. "A backyard campout!" I looked at her and rolled my _____ . "That
                                                                                body part, plural

sounds _____," I replied. But then she promised that we could still pop _____
        adjective   food, plural

and _____ _____ until the _____ came home. Guess it's better than
     verb   noun, plural   animal, plural

staring at a(n) _____ all weekend.
                 noun

friend's name

noun, plural

adjective ending in –est

number

something expensive

room in a house

adjective

type of tree

something found in nature, plural

color

snack, plural

noun

location

favorite singer

noun, plural

adjective

a profession

material

body part

Fun Fact! YOU CAN BUY A TENT SHAPED LIKE THE R.M.S. *TITANIC.*

8

That afternoon, my fellow scouts started to arrive. Suzy Coolidge was crying and _____ (friend's name) was throwing a temper tantrum. Boy, were they bummed out. "Come on, guys! Let's make the best of it!" I said. They dragged their _____ (noun, plural) and tents into the backyard. Suzy's tent was the _____ (adjective ending in –est) thing I had ever seen! It had _____ (number) rooms, a huge _____ (something expensive), and even a(n) _____ (room in a house)! I preferred to be more in touch with nature. I chose a spot under a(n) _____ (adjective) _____ (type of tree), pitched my tiny tent, and gathered a bunch of _____ (something found in nature, plural) to make a bed. When I was finished, we built a campfire. It wasn't long before _____ (color) flames were rising from the logs. We roasted _____ (snack, plural) and sang "The Old _____ (noun) of _____ (location)" by _____ (favorite singer). After sunset, we told scary stories while holding _____ (noun, plural) under our chins. Mine was the best. It was about a(n) _____ (adjective) _____ (a profession) with a(n) _____ (material) _____ (body part). That scared them, all right!

9

Fun Fact! INVENTOR **THOMAS EDISON** BUILT HIS FIRST **LABORATORY** WHEN HE WAS **TEN YEARS OLD.**

- famous astronaut
  - something in the night sky
- noun
  - time of day
- adjective
  - adjective
- noun
  - large number
- something valuable, plural
  - adjective
- noun
  - verb ending in –s
- nonsense word
  - verb ending in –ed
- animal, plural
  - adjective
- something soft

The Genius Awards

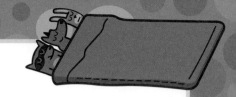

Thanks to earning my _____ badge, I could tell by the position of the _____
famous astronaut   something in the night sky

that it was getting late. I looked at my _____ and saw that it was _____ . The
noun   time of day

other scouts and I decided it was time to turn in. We had a big day ahead. We were going to hold our very

own _____ Genius Awards! Each year at the bonanza, everyone brings an invention. The best one
adjective

wins a(n) _____ _____ and _____ _____ . Since the
adjective   noun   large number   something valuable, plural

bonanza was canceled we were having our own contest. I had been working on my invention all year, and it

was so much better than last year's winner: a(n) _____ _____ that _____
adjective   noun   verb ending in –s

when you say "_____ ." I _____ into my tent and realized I forgot my pillow.
nonsense word   verb ending in –ed

"Oh, _____ ," I whispered. I was too _____ to get up. Fortunately there was
animal, plural   adjective

a(n) _____ nearby, so I used that instead. I closed my eyes and drifted off to sleep.
something soft

- breakfast food, plural
- food, plural
- food, plural
- adjective
- color
- noun
- friend's name
- adjective
- noun
- past-tense verb
- adverb ending in –ly
- friend's name
- noun
- verb
- girl's name
- noun
- silly noise
- silly noise
- past-tense verb

Fun Fact! PLAY-DOH WAS INVENTED TO CLEAN WALLPAPER.

GENIUS AWARDS

When I opened my eyes, the sun was high in the sky. "Today's the day!" Mom said. "Come get some

_____ , then it'll be time for the contest!" I heaped a big pile of _____
　　　breakfast food, plural　　　　　　　　　　　　　　　　　　　　　　　　　　　　　　food, plural

and _____ onto my plate. I gobbled it down as fast as I could and went to retrieve my
　　　　food, plural

invention. To guarantee no one stole my idea, I had hidden it under a(n) _____ _____
　　　　　　　　　　　　　　　　　　　　　　　　　　　　　　　　　　　　adjective　　　　　　　color

_____ in the garden. One by one, my fellow scouts presented their inventions: _____
　　noun　　　friend's name

made a(n) _____ _____ that _____ _____ .
　　　　　　　adjective　　　　　　　noun　　　　　　　　　past-tense verb　　　　adverb ending in –ly

_____ built an entire _____ that could _____ ! But the best by far
　friend's name　　　　　　　　　　　　　　noun　　　　　　　　　　　　　verb

was _____ 's. She made a giant replica of a(n) _____ that actually worked!
　　　　girl's name　　　　　　　　　　　　　　　　　　　　　　　　　noun

The crowd yelled " _____ " and " _____ " as her invention _____
　　　　　　　　　silly noise　　　　　　　　　　silly noise　　　　　　　　　　　　past-tense verb

around the backyard. But little did they know, they hadn't seen anything yet!

- your name
- nickname
- noun, plural
- a profession
- nonsense word
- large number
- adjective
- color
- verb
- friend's name
- same friend's name
- adjective
- adjective
- something shiny
- same nonsense word
- verb
- verb

Fun Fact! SCIENTISTS BUILT A SMALL, SQUISHY **ROBOT** THAT CAN **SQUEEZE** THROUGH TIGHT SPACES THEN **GROW** TEN TIMES ITS ORIGINAL SIZE.

The Greatest Invention of All

"_____ , you're next!" Mom called out. I stepped forward and placed my invention on the ground.
(your name)

Before I could speak, I was interrupted by the telephone. "Go ahead without me, _____ ," Mom said
(nickname)

as she ran off to answer it. Oh well, I thought. I could always show her later. "Ladies and _____ ," I
(noun, plural)

said in my best _____ voice, "I present to you the _____ Shrink Ray _____ !"
(a profession)   (nonsense word)   (large number)

Everyone gasped. A(n) _____ _____ object stood in front of them. "What does it do?"
(adjective)   (color)

someone asked. "It shrinks things!" I replied. I saw the other scouts shake their heads and _____ .
(verb)

"No way!" said _____ . "I'll show you. Please hand me an object to shrink," I said.
(friend's name)

_____ handed over a(n) _____ _____ _____ .
(same friend's name)   (adjective)   (adjective)   (something shiny)

I placed it on the ground and picked up the _____ Shrink Ray. I pointed it directly at the
(same nonsense word)

object. "Ready, _____ , _____ !" I yelled.
(verb)   (verb)

- adjective
  - large object
- body part
  - color
- body part
  - friend's name
- friend's name
  - color
- friend's name
  - color
- adjective
  - something found in nature
- adjective
  - friend's name
- color
  - something tall
- adjective
  - animal
- body part, plural

Fun Fact! ON AVERAGE, **HUMANS** ARE ABOUT **4 INCHES** (10 CM) **TALLER** THAN THEY WERE 100 YEARS AGO.

A Tiny Problem

Suddenly, everything went _____ . I felt like I had been hit by a(n) _____ that knocked
adjective   large object

me on my _____ . When I opened my eyes, all I could see above me was _____ . Where did all
body part   color

the other scouts go? I rubbed my _____ and slowly got to my feet. Next to me, Suzy was on the ground,
body part

too. _____ and _____ were poking their heads out from under giant _____
friend's name   friend's name   color

things, and _____ was laying in a bed of soft _____ things. A few other scouts were lifting
friend's name   color

what appeared to be a(n) _____ _____ off of themselves. The rest peeked out from
adjective   something found in nature

behind _____ -looking green things. "What happened? Where are we?" Suzy asked. "Your shrink
adjective

ray shot us into another dimension!" _____ cried. Just then, I looked up and saw it: my very own
friend's name

tiny _____ tent. Only, it was no longer tiny. It was the size of a(n) _____ ! And then it hit me.
color   something tall

" _____ _____ _____ !" I yelled.
adjective   animal   body part, plural

- type of plant, plural
  - something in a backyard
- something small, plural
  - nonsense word
- color
  - adjective
- verb
  - boy's name
- outdoor sport ending in –ing
  - pet
- verb
  - liquid
- watersport
  - insect, plural
- junk food
  - adjective

Thinking Big

"It actually worked," I said, noticing the giant _____ and a huge _____
                                                    type of plant, plural   something in a backyard

around us. "No it didn't!" Suzy said. "That thing you tried to shrink is right here, and it's still the same size!"

"No, it's not," I said. "It's shrunk. It only seems the same size because we're the size of _____ !"
                                                                                            something small, plural

"Oh my _____ ," Suzy said, her face turning _____ . I looked at my fellow scouts. They
            nonsense word   color

looked _____ , too. I started to _____ away, but then _____ began to list all the
            adjective   verb   boy's name

fun things we could do now that we were small. We could go _____ down an anthill or ride the
                                                              outdoor sport ending in –ing

_____ just for fun. We could _____ down the garden hose into puddles of _____ !
      pet   verb   liquid

We could _____ in the rain barrel and keep _____ as pets! And
            watersport   insect, plural

if we could make it back to our campsite, just one _____ would be
                                                       junk food

a(n) _____ feast!
         adjective

19

adjective

    something sharp

body part

    school subject

noun

    noun, plural

nonsense word

    adjective

vacation destination

    verb ending in –ing

adjective

    verb ending in –ing

verb

    adjective

animal

    body part

verb

    body part

Fun Fact! THE WORLD-FAMOUS **WIMBLEDON** TENNIS CHAMPIONSHIP IS PLAYED ON A **GRASS COURT.**

The list of _____ things we could do now that we were tiny was tempting, but what about a trip to
                    adjective

the doctor's office? The _____ would be bigger than my _____ ! And forget
                        something sharp   body part

about taking a(n) _____ test. How can you get an A if you can't lift a(n) _____ ?
                    school subject   noun

But I had a plan. All we needed to do was get to the shed, where I left my _____ . I could
                                                                            noun, plural

simply fiddle with the _____ panel and zap us back to normal. The _____ shed
                        nonsense word   adjective

seemed as far away as _____ , but we had no choice. We set out, _____
                        vacation destination   verb ending in –ing

around _____ blades of grass and _____ over pebbles. At one point, we all had to
        adjective   verb ending in –ing

_____ over a(n) _____ _____ hole! We were making good time, when some-
    verb   adjective   animal

thing grabbed my _____ . I tried to _____ , but then I felt it grip my _____ .
                    body part   verb   body part

I tried to take another step forward but was stopped by an invisible force. I was caught in a spiderweb!

- verb ending in –ing
  - adjective
- noun, plural
  - adjective beginning with the letter "S"
- adjective
  - mealtime
- exclamation
  - adjective
- number
  - color
- adjective
  - adjective
- number
  - body part, plural
- body part, plural
  - past-tense verb
- past-tense verb

Fun Fact! SPIDERS SECRETE SILK FROM THEIR ABDOMENS.

"Oh _____ _____ _____!" I muttered under my breath. How would
       verb ending in –ing   *adjective*   *noun, plural*

I get out of this mess? I knew enough from earning my _____ Spider badge
                                                    adjective beginning with the letter "S"

that spiders don't usually just abandon their _____ webs. Some species set them up and
                                                adjective

wait for unsuspecting _____ to get stuck. The last thing I needed was to end up as spider
                       mealtime

chow! I heard the other scouts yell, "_____!" I looked around and saw my worst fear
                                        exclamation

staring back at me: eight _____ legs, _____ _____ eyes, and two
                           adjective   *number*   *color*

very _____ fangs. The creature was _____ and at least _____ times my
      adjective   *adjective*   *number*

size. I moved my _____ and my _____ ... but I couldn't free myself.
                  body part, plural   *body part, plural*

I _____ and _____ , but I didn't even budge. I was doomed!
   past-tense verb   *past-tense verb*

adverb

   number

noun, plural

   noun

number

   noun, plural

nonsense word

   a profession

verb ending in –ing

   command

adjective

   liquid

body part, plural

   adjective

something found inside your body

   body part

verb

Fun Fact! SOME SPECIES OF **SPIDERS,** KNOWN AS "SOCIAL SPIDERS," **HUNT** IN PACKS.

In the Nick of Time

Suddenly, someone shouted, "Scouts, take out your packs, _____ !" Our packs! I had completely
adverb

forgotten we were wearing our packs! Every scout is issued a pack with _____ _____ , a(n)
number _noun, plural_

_____ , _____ pairs of _____ , and the _____ _____
noun _number_ _noun, plural_ _nonsense word_ _a profession_

scissors. I couldn't reach mine, but everyone else took out their scissors and started _____ the
verb ending in –ing

web. " _____ !" I yelled. "It's closing in!" I looked up and saw the spider right over me.
command

Its _____ fangs were dripping _____ onto my face. The spider rubbed its back
adjective _liquid_

_____ together, preparing to wrap me in a cocoon of _____ thread and
body part, plural _adjective_

suck my _____ from my body. I raised my _____ to shield my eyes ...
something found inside your body _body part_

and realized that I was free! The other scouts had rescued me! "All right, everybody ... _____ !"
verb

I yelled as I was pulled to safety just in time.

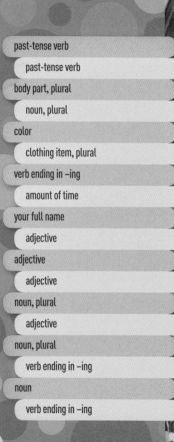

past-tense verb

past-tense verb

body part, plural

noun, plural

color

clothing item, plural

verb ending in –ing

amount of time

your full name

adjective

adjective

adjective

noun, plural

adjective

noun, plural

verb ending in –ing

noun

verb ending in –ing

Fun Fact! LYNDON B. JOHNSON WAS THE ONLY U.S. **PRESIDENT** TO HAVE TAKEN THE OATH OF OFFICE ON AN **AIRPLANE.**

The Official Oath

The scouts and I _____ and _____ as fast as our _____ could carry
_____ (past-tense verb) _____ (past-tense verb) _____ (body part, plural)

us. Finally, totally out of breath, I stopped. "Let's rest here on these _____," I said, pointing to the
_____ (noun, plural)

tiny _____ objects growing out of the ground. I sat down and took off my _____. My
_____ (color) _____ (clothing item, plural)

fellow scouts did the same. We were all exhausted. We had been _____ for _____,
_____ (verb ending in –ing) _____ (amount of time)

and we didn't seem to be getting very far. "This is pointless!" cried Suzy. "It's going to take us days to reach the

shed!" "Don't think like that, we'll find a way," I replied. "Remember our scout oath: I, _____,
_____ (your full name)

solemnly swear to be _____, _____, and _____, to offer
_____ (adjective) _____ (adjective) _____ (adjective)

_____ to those in need, to be _____ in the face of _____, and to never
_____ (noun, plural) _____ (adjective) _____ (noun, plural)

stop _____ for the _____." Everyone began to perk up. That seemed to do the trick.
_____ (verb ending in –ing) _____ (noun)

"Come on, scouts," I said. "We're _____ time!"
_____ (verb ending in –ing)

Fun Fact!

RAIN FORESTS
ARE HOME TO MORE
ANIMAL SPECIES
THAN ANY OTHER HABITAT.

- adjective
  - type of plant
- adjective
  - noun, plural
- noun, plural
  - exotic landscape
- adjective
  - adjective
- animal, plural
  - favorite toy
- board game
  - past-tense verb
- adjective ending in –est
  - noun
- number
  - clothing item, plural

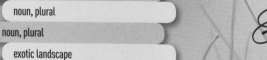

It's a Jungle Out There

It wasn't too long before I realized we were lost. Every now and then, someone would climb a(n) _____
_____ adjective

_____ to make sure we were staying on course, but the grass was getting _____ and
_____type of plant_____ _____adjective_____

we couldn't see beyond the _____ and the _____ . The backyard was like a(n)
_____noun, plural_____ _____noun, plural_____

_____ , and I got the feeling that we were unwelcome by the natives. We had already escaped
_____exotic landscape_____

that _____ spider, and I did not want to encounter any _____ bugs, not to mention
_____adjective_____ _____adjective_____

any dangerous _____ . But I did find my childhood _____ and half of the missing
_____animal, plural_____ _____favorite toy_____

pieces to _____ . Suddenly, we _____ in our tracks. In front of us was the
_____board game_____ _____past-tense verb_____

_____ mountain I had ever seen. It was actually a(n) _____ , but at our size that
_____adjective ending in –est_____ _____noun_____

was really the same thing. We had no choice but to climb it. It could take _____ hours to go around!
_____number_____

"Scouts, take off your _____ ," I said. "I have a plan!"
_____clothing item, plural_____

famous explorer

   adjective

famous mountain

   type of dessert

number

   same number

clothing item, plural

   adjective

something long

   shape

same something long

   adverb ending in –ly

past-tense verb

   adjective

adjective

   something gross, plural

number

   name of a large body of water

Fun Fact! **MOUNT EVEREST** IS ROUGHLY THE HEIGHT OF **1,528 GIRAFFES** STACKED ON TOP OF ONE ANOTHER.

Marching Up the Mountain

I imagined myself as _____ , scaling the _____ slopes of _____ .
famous explorer _adjective_ _famous mountain_

Surely this would be a piece of _____ . _____ by _____ , the
type of dessert _number_ _same number_

scouts handed me their _____ . I tied them together to create a(n) _____
clothing item, plural _adjective_

_____ . Next we formed a human _____ . I climbed to the very top, hoisted
something long _shape_

myself up onto the peak of the rock, and lowered down the _____ . _____ ,
same something long _adverb ending in –ly_

I _____ each scout to the top. Boy, were they _____ ! When the last scout was
past-tense verb _adjective_

pulled to safety, I surveyed the land. " _____ _____ !" I said. We were a lot
adjective _something gross, plural_

farther away from the shed than I thought. At our size, it would take _____ days to get there! But even
number

worse, when I looked down, there was a mud puddle the size of _____ ! We needed a plan.
name of a large body of water

31

adverb ending in –ly

adjective

texture

adjective

verb ending in –ing

funny noise

color

adjective

noun, plural

planet

adjective

food

noun

verb

friend's name

vehicle

last name

swim move

animal

Fun Fact! THE **ONLY** EVENT IN THE FIRST **13 OLYMPIC GAMES** WAS A SHORT RUNNING RACE.

Mudlympics

Very _____ , we scooted our way down the mountain. We were lucky that there were
adverb ending in –ly

_____ ridges for us to grip so that we didn't fall. Suddenly, the ridges stopped. The surface was
adjective

completely _____ . Even worse ... it was _____ from rain! Before I could call a warning
texture   *adjective*

to the other scouts, I lost my grip and ... *Whooosh!* We went _____ down the side of the mountain,
verb ending in –ing

and _____ —landed right in the mud. Everyone was neck-deep in the sticky _____ stuff.
funny noise   *color*

I couldn't help but laugh. We looked like _____ _____ from _____ .
adjective   *noun, plural*   *planet*

"All right, scouts!" I called. "Mudlympics! Last one to the other side is a(n) _____ _____ !"
adjective   *food*

Suzy Coolidge picked up a(n) _____ and began to _____ across the lake. _____
noun   *verb*   *friend's name*

found a giant leaf, made it into a(n) _____ shape, and began to paddle. The _____ twins
vehicle   *last name*

were doing the _____ . I was trying my best just to keep up by _____ -paddling.
swim move   *animal*

- adjective
  - food
- something large
  - noun
- time of day
  - noun
- large number
  - something metal, plural
- machine
  - body part, plural
- color
  - adjective
- adjective
  - something sharp
- something found in nature
  - verb ending in –ing

Fun Fact! HONEYBEES HAVE A SEPARATE STOMACH JUST FOR HONEY.

Attack of the Killer Bee

By now I was _____ and hungry. I swear I could have eaten a(n) _____ the size of
                    adjective   food

a(n) _____! I looked at my _____ to check the time. It was _____,
        something large   noun   time of day

and I was really worried about reaching the shed before dark. I started to climb up a(n) _____ to
                                                                                              noun

check our distance, but I fell back to the ground, rattled by the loudest racket I've ever heard. It sounded

like _____ _____ being put into a(n) _____! I covered
        large number   something metal, plural   machine

my _____ and ran. A(n) _____ shadow fell over me. I looked up and saw the most
      body part, plural   color

terrifying sight of my life: a(n) _____ _____ bee with a stinger that looked
                                      adjective   adjective

just like a(n) _____. I dove for cover under a(n) _____. The other scouts
                  something sharp   something found in nature

followed. The bee was _____ closer. Then it landed on the ground—right in front of us!
                          verb ending in –ing

- number
  - verb
- verb
  - past-tense verb
- noun
  - body part, plural
- same body part, plural
  - adverb ending in –ly
- verb
  - adjective beginning with the letter "B"
- past-tense verb
  - dance move
- dance move
  - verb ending in –ing
- insect
  - nonsense word
- verb

Fun Fact! FEMALE HONEYBEES PERFORM A "WAGGLE" DANCE WHEN THEY FIND A NECTAR SOURCE.

Speaking Their Language

For the next _____ minutes, the bee didn't _____. I decided I would scare it off. Bees hate
          number   _verb_

when you _____ at them. I _____ out from under my _____ and waved
              verb   _past-tense verb_   _noun_

my _____ in the air. The bee came closer. I waved my _____ even more. It wasn't
     body part, plural   _same body part, plural_

working! Finally, I wiggled my whole body to try to get the bee to back off. _____, the bee began
                                                                          adverb ending in –ly

to _____ back! Then I remembered something from when I earned my _____
       verb   _adjective beginning with the letter "B"_

Bee badge. Bees communicate with each other by "dancing" in the direction of a food source. If I danced in the

direction of the shed, would the bee understand? Could it help us get to the shed? I _____ closer.
                                                                                   past-tense verb

I did the _____ and pointed to the shed. Nothing. So I tried the _____, followed by
           dance move   _dance move_

the _____ man, the _____, and the _____ pokey. Still nothing. The bee
    verb ending in –ing   _insect_   _nonsense word_

flew off. Oh well, at least it didn't _____ me.
                                          verb

adverb ending in –ly

natural disaster

verb

body part, plural

adjective

color

shape

adjective

adjective

noun, plural

body part

color

number

number

number

name of a group of animals

something large

name of a group of animals, plural

Fun Fact! PILL BUGS ARE CRUSTACEANS, LIKE CRABS AND LOBSTERS.

We continued on our journey. We hadn't gotten too far when suddenly, the ground started shaking

_____ . "_____ !" I yelled. My mind raced as I tried to remember what my scout guide said
adverb ending in –ly   natural disaster

to do in this situation. "Everybody, _____ to the ground!" Everyone dropped to their _____ as
                                              verb   body part, plural

the shaking grew more and more _____ . Suddenly, a huge _____ _____ came
                                                  adjective   color   shape

rolling toward me. "_____ _____ _____ !" I yelled. "What is that?" The shape
                              adjective   adjective   noun, plural

stopped a few feet away from me, and a little _____ popped up. A pill bug! Several more shapes
                                                            body part

came rolling in. Above us, the sky turned _____ . I looked up and saw a swarm of nearly _____
                                                      color   number

bees, _____ ladybugs, and _____ butterflies fill the sky. A(n) _____ of worms as
            number   number   name of a group of animals

big as a(n) _____ wiggled up from the ground, and _____ of beetles and
                  something large   name of a group of animals, plural

ants surrounded us from behind. We're in trouble now, I thought.

- verb ending in –ed
- direction
- direction
- friend's name
- type of plant, plural
- boy's name
- noun, plural
- kind of flower
- something found in nature
- past-tense verb
- insect body part
- noun
- adjective
- adjective
- number
- school subject

To the Rescue

The scouts _____ _____ and _____ . _____ hid in a
      verb ending in –ed   _direction_   _direction_   _friend's name_

group of _____ . _____ covered himself in _____ . Three or
   type of plant, plural   _boy's name_   _noun, plural_

four people hid behind a large _____ . And the rest dove under a(n) _____ .
                                  kind of flower   _something found in nature_

That left just me and Suzy out in the open to fend for ourselves. Suddenly, a bee swooped down from the

sky and _____ in front of us. It began to wiggle its _____ . I picked up a small
         past-tense verb   _insect body part_

_____ . "Look, you seem like a(n) _____ insect, but I'll throw this if I have to," I warned
   noun   _adjective_

the bee. "It doesn't want to hurt us," Suzy said. "I think it wants to help us! And I think these other bugs are

friends!" Normally, I would have thought Suzy was _____ , but she had _____ badges
                                                     adjective   _number_

in bug _____ , so she knew far more than me. "Okay ... I guess there's only one way to find out,"
        school subject

I said. "Come on, scouts! Find a bug and climb aboard!"

41

adjective

   insect body part, plural

adverb ending in –ly

   fast vehicle

amusement park ride

   noun, plural

noun, plural

   pet's name

noun, plural

   noun

something bright, plural

   flying insect, plural

crawling insect, plural

   large animal, plural

adverb ending in –ly

Fun Fact! BEES BEAT THEIR WINGS ABOUT **230 TIMES** PER SECOND.

On the Back of a Bee

I grabbed on to the bee's _____ hair and hoisted myself up. The bee beat its _____
    (adjective)   (insect body part, plural)

_____ , and we were soon in flight. It was like nothing I'd ever experienced before. Kind
(adverb ending in –ly)

of like a(n) _____ ride and a(n) _____ rolled into one. We dipped and dove
              (fast vehicle)   (amusement park ride)

over _____ and _____ . A quick trip over the yard revealed my dog _____
      (noun, plural)   (noun, plural)   (pet's name)

burying his/her _____ in the _____ . On either side of us, butterflies accompanied us
                  (noun, plural)   (noun)

on our journey like our own personal _____ . On _____ nearby, I saw Suzy
                                        (something bright, plural)   (flying insect, plural)

and a few other scouts. Below me the stragglers were racing to catch up on the backs of _____ ,
                                                                                            (crawling insect, plural)

holding on for dear life like they were riding wild _____ . A short while later, the shed
                                                      (large animal, plural)

was right below us. The bee _____ came in for a landing and dropped me off at the door.
                              (adverb ending in –ly)

"Thanks for the ride!" I called. "I owe you one!"

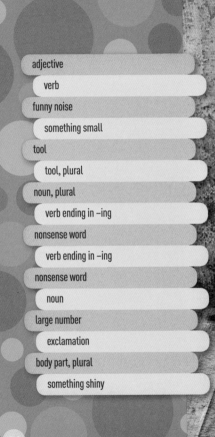

- adjective
  - verb
- funny noise
  - something small
- tool
  - tool, plural
- noun, plural
  - verb ending in –ing
- nonsense word
  - verb ending in –ing
- nonsense word
  - noun
- large number
  - exclamation
- body part, plural
  - something shiny

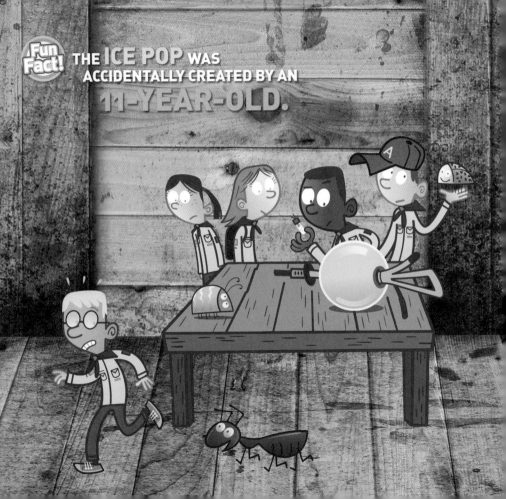

Even with all of us pushing, the door to the shed was too _____ to open. Good thing we were small

adjective

enough to _____ under! "My tools!" I shouted when I finally saw the workbench in front of me. I pulled

verb

out my shrink ray and aimed it at the bench. 1 ... 2 ... 3 ... _____! The workbench shrank down to

funny noise

the size of a(n) _____. I picked up my _____, a few _____, and

something small tool tool, plural

some _____ for good measure. I fiddled with the control panel to rejigger the settings, which

noun, plural

required _____ the _____ switch and _____ the _____

verb ending in –ing nonsense word verb ending in –ing nonsense word

settings. I aimed it at a nearby _____ and zapped it. It grew _____ times its size.

noun large number

"_____!" I said. Perhaps I went a little overboard. I adjusted the settings and zapped it again. "That

exclamation

oughta do it!" I said. "Ready, scouts?" They eagerly nodded their _____. We gathered in a group and

body part, plural

aimed the shrink ray at the _____ in front of us. 1 ... 2 ... 3!

something shiny

body part, plural

    adjective

exclamation

    number

verb ending in –ed

    verb ending in –ing

adverb ending in –ly

    adjective

favorite snack, plural

    favorite candy

adjective

    number

same number

    color

animal

    nonsense word, plural

adjective

Fun Fact! THE EARLIEST PIZZA DATES BACK TO THE SIXTH CENTURY B.C.

A New Friend

I opened my _____ and looked around. I was _____ enough to see out the
   body part, plural   _adjective_

window. "_____!" I yelled. "We're back to normal size." Everyone high-_____-ed and
      exclamation   _number_

_____ for joy. Just then, Mom walked in. "Here you guys are! I've been _____
verb ending in –ed   _verb ending in –ing_

everywhere for you! Have you been in the shed the whole time?" I _____ nodded with a(n)
                                                                          adverb ending in –ly

_____ grin on my face. "Well, I ordered a couple of _____ and _____
      adjective   _favorite snack, plural_   _favorite candy_

pizzas. You must be _____! Come eat!" She had no idea. We shuffled out of the shed
                          adjective

_____ by _____. As I turned around to lock the door, I saw something _____
      number   _same number_   _color_

about the size of a(n) _____ move inside. I opened the door back up to find the world's largest bee
                              animal

buzzing around inside the shed. "Aw, _____!" I said, laughing to myself. "Mom's not gonna
                                            nonsense word, plural

like this." I shut the door and went inside to get my _____ friend a slice of pizza.
                                                            adjective

Credits

Cover, Close Encounters Photo/Shutterstock; 4, Room27/Shutterstock; 6, Artazum and Iriana Shiyan/Shutterstock; 8, Artazum and Iriana Shiyan/Shutterstock; 10, Jesse Kunerth/Shutterstock; 12, Varuna/Shutterstock; 14, Kim Doucette/Shutterstock; 16, Linda George/Shutterstock; 18, Andrey Armyagov/Shutterstock; 20, Aris Suwanmalee/Shutterstock; 22, Aleksey Stemmer/Shutterstock; 24, Stefano Garau/Shutterstock; 26, Aaragami12345s/Shutterstock; 28, Andrey Armyagov/Shutterstock; 30, Muangsatun/Shutterstock; 32, Majaan/Shutterstock; 34, Noah Golan/Shutterstock; 36, Alix Kreil/Shutterstock; 38, Mauro Rodrigues/Shutterstock; 40, Pakhnyushcha/Shutterstock; 42, Jaan-Martin Kuusmann/Shutterstock; 44, Hannamariah/Shutterstock; 46, photogress/iStock.

Published by the National Geographic Society

Gary E. Knell, *President and Chief Executive Officer*
John M. Fahey, *Chairman of the Board*
Declan Moore, *Executive Vice President; President, Publishing and Travel*
Melina Gerosa Bellows, *Publisher; Chief Creative Officer, Books, Kids, and Family*

Prepared by the Book Division

Hector Sierra, *Senior Vice President and General Manager*
Nancy Laties Feresten, *Senior Vice President, Kids Publishing and Media*
Jennifer Emmett, *Vice President, Editorial Director, Kids Books*
Eva Absher-Schantz, *Design Director, Kids Publishing and Media*
Jay Sumner, *Director of Photography, Kids Publishing*
R. Gary Colbert, *Production Director*
Jennifer A. Thornton, *Director of Managing Editorial*

Staff for This Book

Shelby Alinsky, *Project Editor*
James Hiscott, Jr., *Art Director*
Kelley Miller, *Senior Photo Editor*
Becky Baines, *Writer*
Jim Paillot, *Illustrator*
Paige Towler, *Editorial Assistant*
Allie Allen, Sanjida Rashid, *Design Production Assistants*
Margaret Leist, *Photo Assistant*
Grace Hill, *Associate Managing Editor*
Joan Gossett, *Production Editor*
Lewis R. Bassford, *Production Manager*
Susan Borke, *Legal and Business Affairs*

Production Services

Phillip L. Schlosser, *Senior Vice President*
Chris Brown, *Vice President, NG Book Manufacturing*
George Bounelis, *Senior Production Manager*
Nicole Elliott, *Director of Production*
Rachel Faulise, *Manager*
Robert L. Barr, *Manager*

Editorial, Design, and Production by Plan B Book Packagers

The National Geographic Society is one of the world's largest nonprofit scientific and educational organizations. Founded in 1888 to "increase and diffuse geographic knowledge," the Society's mission is to inspire people to care about the planet. It reaches more than 400 million people worldwide each month through its official journal, *National Geographic*, and other magazines; National Geographic Channel; television documentaries; music; radio; films; books; DVDs; maps; exhibitions; live events; school publishing programs; interactive media; and merchandise. National Geographic has funded more than 10,000 scientific research, conservation, and exploration projects and supports an education program promoting geographic literacy.

For more information, please call 1-800-NGS LINE (647-5463) or write to the following address:

National Geographic Society, 1145 17th Street N.W., Washington, D.C. 20036-4688 U.S.A.

Visit us online at nationalgeographic.com/books

For librarians and teachers: ngchildrensbooks.org

More for kids from National Geographic: kids.nationalgeographic.com

For information about special discounts for bulk purchases, please contact National Geographic Books Special Sales: ngspecsales@ngs.org

For rights or permissions inquiries, please contact National Geographic Books Subsidiary Rights: ngbookrights@ngs.org

ISBN: 978-1-4263-1738-5

Printed in Hong Kong

14/THK/1